Dear Readers,

This is the story of a little girl who was happy with her family and friends in Senegambia, Africa. But one day her life changed forever, and she became sad. It was then that she began writing poetry. Writing made her feel wonderful.

In this book you will meet this girl. Her name is Phillis Wheatley. Sometimes you might want to try writing when you feel sad, or happy, or scared. Put your thoughts on paper. You may be able to write poems, too.

Your friend,

Garnet Jackson

Phillis Wheatley
Poet

Written by Garnet Nelson Jackson
Illustrated by Cheryl Hanna

 MODERN CURRICULUM PRESS

Program Reviewers

Maureen Besst, Teacher
  Orange County Public Schools
  Orlando, Florida

Carol Brown, Director of Reading
  Freeport Schools
  Freeport, New York

Kanani Choy, Principal
  Clarendon Alternative School
  San Francisco, California

Barbara Jackson-Nash, Deputy Director
  Banneker-Douglass Museum
  Annapolis, Maryland

Minesa Taylor, Teacher
  Mayfair Elementary School
  East Cleveland, Ohio

MODERN CURRICULUM PRESS
13900 Prospect Road, Cleveland, Ohio 44136
Simon & Schuster • A Paramount Communications Company

Copyright © 1993 Modern Curriculum Press, Inc.

Library of Congress Catalog Card Number: 92-28778
ISBN 0-8136-5233-2 (Reinforced Binding)   ISBN 0-8136-5706-7 (Paperback)

10 9 8 7 6 5 4   97 96 95 94

Text Printed on Recycled Paper

A sunbeam fell across the face of a little girl sleeping in her home in West Africa. The sunbeam gave bright colors to her dreams just before her eyes opened.

Fatou rose and twirled happily in the sun's rays, as she did every morning. Through the window, she saw her mother stretch out on the dew-covered grass. This was a Muslim way of greeting the new day.

3

Later, as Fatou and her friends
played outside their village, she ran
off too far. Suddenly she was
grabbed and dragged far from her
village. She was kidnapped !

Fatou spent many days in the bottom of an awful ship. It carried its load of kidnapped children and grown-ups across the Atlantic Ocean to America. In those long-ago days, some African people were sold in America as slaves. Slaves had to work for their owners all their lives without pay.

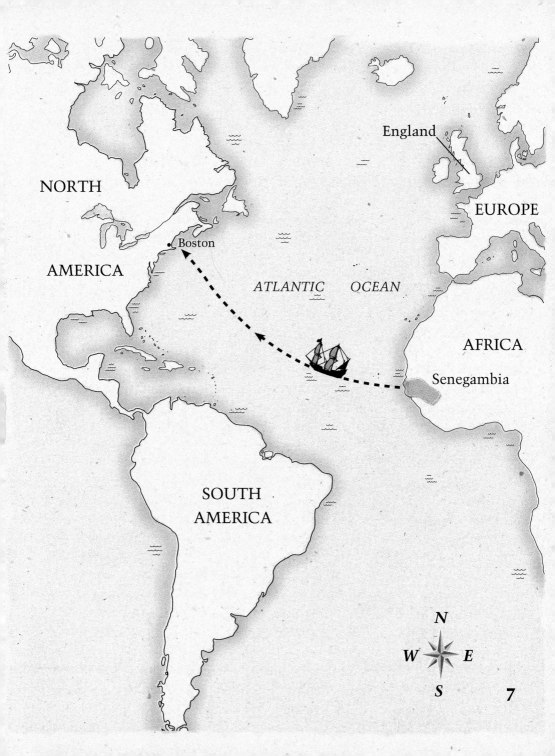

NORTH

AMERICA

Boston

England

EUROPE

ATLANTIC   OCEAN

AFRICA

Senegambia

SOUTH
AMERICA

N
W ✸ *E*
S

7

8

Fatou was taken from the ship to the slave market in the city of Boston. There Mrs. Susannah Wheatley bought Fatou to be her slave girl. She changed Fatou's name to "Phillis."

Phillis learned English quickly.
Mrs. Wheatley saw how smart Phillis
was. She allowed her own teen-aged
children, Mary and Nat, to teach
Phillis to read. Soon Phillis taught
herself to write.

Learning how to read and write
made Phillis different because most
slaves were not allowed to do these
things. Many slave-owners did not
want slaves to know very much. But
the Wheatleys allowed Phillis to
read their books and gave her paper
and pens for writing.

Although Phillis was treated kindly
by her new family, the scary
adventures of her past often made
her sad.

At times she felt very
lonely in her
new home.

13

But she liked reading and learning.
Writing, in particular, always made
her smile. She loved to write
poems.

When Phillis wrote, she shared her
ideas and wishes. She visited
places she could have only
dreamed of. She was able to
invent places and make them what
she wanted them to be.

15

16

17

NORTH

AMERICA

• Boston

ATLANTIC OCEAN

England

EUROPE

AFRICA

Senegambia

N
W E
S

18

As Phillis grew up, she wrote more and more beautiful poems. When she was only 15, she wrote a poem to the King of England!

Two years later, the first collection of her poetry was published in America. She was becoming a famous poet.

A few years later, Phillis visited England. There, lords and ladies wanted to meet the young woman who wrote so beautifully.
When a complete book of her poems was published in England, Phillis became the second American woman to have a book published.

After she returned to America, Phillis was freed. She met a wonderful man, fell in love, and married.

23

Even though she lived nearly 200 years ago, Phillis Wheatley is remembered today as one of America's important poets.

Glossary

colony (käl′ ə nē) *plural **colonies*** A group of people who live in one country but are ruled by another country from which they came

Fatou (fa tu′) A person's name from Senegal, Africa, which means "brilliant"; it may have been Phillis Wheatley's African name.

lady (lād′ ē) *plural **ladies*** 1. A woman, especially a polite woman. 2. A special title for a woman who belongs to an important family.

lord (lôrd) A person with power, a master

Muslim (muz′ lim *or* mooz′ lim) A word describing people or things that are part of the religion of Islam

Senegambia (sen′ i gam′ bē a) A country in west Africa that no longer exists; it was made up of lands that are in the modern countries of Senegal and Gambia.

About the Author

Garnet Jackson is an elementary teacher in Flint, Michigan, with a deep concern for developing a positive self-image in young African American students. After an unsuccessful search for materials about famous African Americans written on the level of early readers, Ms. Jackson filled the gap by producing a series of biographies herself. In addition to being a teacher, Ms. Jackson is a poet and a newspaper columnist. She has one son, Damon. She dedicates this book to the memory of her dear mother, Carrie Sherman.

About the Illustrator

Cheryl Hanna, a native of Michigan, has worked as a commercial artist for twenty years and is also a designer and teacher. Ms. Hanna has illustrated several other books, including *An Enchanted Hair Tail*, which won the 1987 ALA Notable Book Award. In *Phillis Wheatley,* her artistic composition and use of oil wash and pastel pencils place the reader in the midst of a cultural journey that encompasses both the African and the American experience.